BAT

by *CAROLINE ARNOLD*
photographs by **RICHARD HEWETT**
MORROW JUNIOR BOOKS • New York

PHOTO CREDITS: Permission to use the following photographs is gratefully acknowledged: M. Brock Fenton, pages 28 (bottom), 31, 37, 39; Gary McCracken, pages 32–33, 41; Arthur Arnold, page 43 (bottom).

The text type is 14-point Palatino.

Library of Congress Cataloging-in-Publication Data   Arnold, Caroline.   Bat/by Caroline Arnold; photographs by Richard Hewett.   p. cm. Includes index.   Summary: Discusses the physiology and behavior of this mammal as well as the fears, misconceptions, and superstitions that have given it a bad reputation.   ISBN 0-688-13726-1 (trade)—ISBN 0-688-13727-X (library)   1. Bats—Juvenile literature.   [1. Bats.] I. Hewett, Richard, ill.   II. Title.   QL737.C5A77 1996   599.4—dc20   95-35228   CIP   AC

ACKNOWLEDGMENTS

We are extremely grateful to Diana Simons (pictured above) and the Wildlife Center in San Diego, California, for their cheerful cooperation and for helping us learn more about bats. We also thank M. Brock Fenton, York University, Canada, and Gary McCracken, University of Tennessee, for their photographs of bats, and Dr. Fenton for his expert reading of the manuscript. Thanks also to BBH Exhibits, Inc., and "Masters of the Night: The True Story of Bats"; the Natural History Museum of Los Angeles County in Burbank, California; and Bat Conservation International, Austin, Texas. For additional assistance, we thank Al Kisner; Kris Mashburn; the Los Angeles Zoo; the Living Desert Museum, in Palm Desert, California; and the National Park Service at Carlsbad Caverns, New Mexico. We are grateful to Ann Garrett and Don Jim for their special help, and, as always, we thank our editor, Andrea Curley, for her continued support.

You can write to Bat Conservation International at P.O. Box 162603, Austin, Texas 78716 to find out about bat conservation worldwide and how you can help bats where you live.

Mexican free-tailed bat.

After a day of resting, a bat wakes up and looks around. As it extends its limbs, the thin skin between the bones stretches tight to form the broad flight surface of the bat's wings. Despite their delicate appearance, the wings are strong and flexible and enable the bat to be an expert flier. Soon the bat will take off into the night, swooping and diving like an aerial acrobat as it searches for the insects that are its food.

The control of some insect pests is fit from having bats around. Yet because they do not know much about them, most people do not appreciate bats, and some species are threatened or endangered.

You may have seen the dark graceful shapes of bats silhouetted against the sky on a warm summer evening. Bats are fascinating animals that are extremely good at getting around at night and in the air. As we learn more about bats, we will be better able to protect them and the places where

Bats are found throughout North America. Although some bats live close to people, most spend their whole lives without ever having direct contact with humans. Sometimes, however, bats are hurt by other animals, by people, or in accidental collisions. In many communities there are people who are trained to care for injured bats safely and help bring them back to health. Usually the bats can be released to the wild after they recover, but in some cases, if the bats can no longer fend for themselves, they continue to get human care.

Tad and Gus were injured bats that were found and cared for by people working with the Wildlife Center, an organization in southern California that rescues bats and other hurt wild animals. Tad and Gus are frequently taken to visit schools and community groups to help people learn more about bats. They provide an opportunity for people to see how tiny most bats are and to appreciate some of their special features. Although each bat species is unique, all of them have things in common, including the amazing ability to fly.

Big brown bat.

Gus is a big brown bat, one of the most widespread bat species in North America. This species is also found in northern South America and on the islands of the West Indies, in the Caribbean. Big brown bats are often found inside buildings and are among the most commonly seen bats in larger cities. They are also found in wooded and semiopen areas.

The big brown bat is a small- to medium-size bat with a body weight of .42 to .84 ounce (12 to 24 grams). It has broad wings and small black ears, and its fur color ranges from tan to dark brown. As with most bat species, male and female big brown bats have similar coloring.

Tad is a Mexican free-tailed bat, a common species in the southern and southwestern United States and in Mexico and Central America. Mexican free-tails live inside hollow trees and buildings, and in crevices on the outsides of buildings and other structures. They are also found in caves and often congregate in huge colonies. Bracken Cave in Texas is the home of 20 million Mexican free-tailed bats. Carlsbad Caverns in New Mexico and the Congress Avenue Bridge in Austin, Texas, are some other famous sites for this species.

The Mexican free-tailed bat is small, with a coat of short chocolate brown fur, a wrinkled upper lip, and small ears that lie flat across the top of the head. An adult weighs about .42 to .53 ounce (12 to 15 grams). With both Mexican free-tailed bats and big brown bats, males are usually slightly smaller than females.

Mexican free-tailed bat.

A big brown bat is actually quite small.

FALSE BELIEFS ABOUT BATS

Superstitions and false ideas about bats have given them a bad reputation. Because bats are active mainly at night and live in secluded places, they are often misunderstood and feared. Most bats are gentle and shy and do not attack people or other animals. If a bat accidentally flies into a building, you should open the doors and windows so it can get out.

Contrary to popular belief, bats do not try to get tangled in your hair. Bats sometimes swoop close overhead in pursuit of insects, but they are skillful fliers and can easily avoid bumping into people.

Perhaps the most dangerous misconception is that bats have rabies and carry diseases. Bats, just like any other mammal, can get rabies, but the danger of a person getting rabies from a bat is extremely small. Many people also believe that bats are rabies carriers, which would mean that they could give rabies to others without suffering from the symptoms themselves. This is not true either. If a bat gets rabies, it dies quietly and rarely becomes aggressive.

The idea that bats are rabies carriers began because of some studies done many years ago with bats that had Rio Bravo virus, a harmless disease that produces symptoms similar to those of rabies. The bats recovered, and this led to the false conclusion that bats could survive rabies and become carriers. Unfortunately, before the mistake was discovered, this idea spread widely, and even today many people still believe it.

Rabies spreads when an infected animal bites another animal. The rabies germs get into the bloodstream from the saliva of the sick animal's bite. People who work with injured bats wear sturdy gloves until they can determine that the bat is safe to handle without them. If you find an injured bat or any other wild animal, don't handle it—all animals will bite in self-defense if they feel threatened. Instead, call the department of animal control in your community.

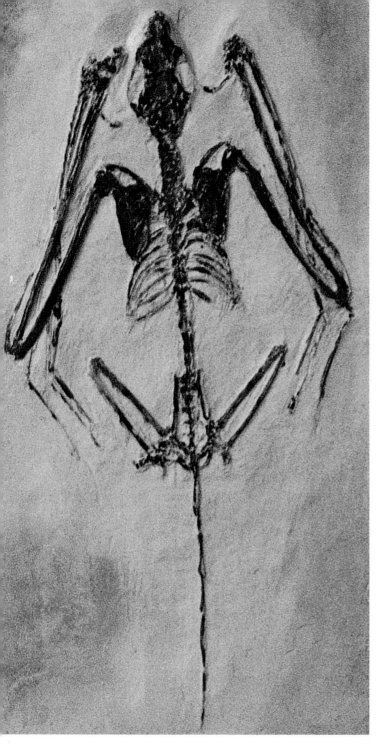
Fifty-million-year-old bat fossil found in Wyoming.

THE FIRST BATS

In ancient times people thought that bats were some kind of strange, furry bird. Today we know that bats are not birds at all, but mammals, just like dogs, cats, and people. (Mammals are animals that have fur or hair and feed their babies milk.) Bats are the only mammals that fly. A few other mammals—flying squirrels, marsupial sugar gliders, and the colugo, or flying lemur—have winglike flaps of skin between their arms and legs that enable them to glide from tree to tree, but those animals cannot propel themselves through the air in true flight as bats can.

Bats have been around for at least 50 million years and may have been flying in night skies at the same time that the last dinosaurs walked the earth, 65 million years ago. Fossils of prehistoric bats have been found on every continent except Antarctica. Fossil skeletons of the earliest bats reveal a bone structure amazingly similar to that of modern bats. The fossilized bones are also thin and lightweight, and the limbs are well adapted for flight.

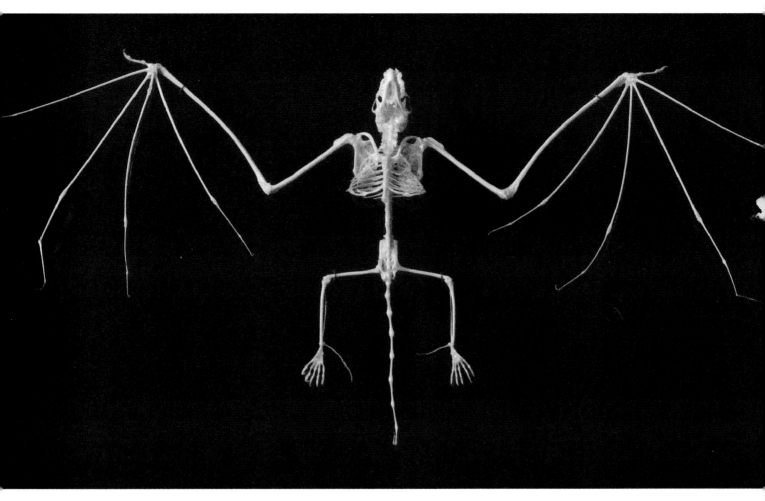

Skeleton of a little brown bat.

There are more than 950 species of bats in the world today. Except for rodents, no other group of mammals includes such a wide variety of species. Bats are a highly diverse group of animals and range in size from the tiny hog-nosed bat of Thailand, with a weight of less than .1 ounce (2.9 grams) and a wingspan of about 6 inches (15.4 centimeters), to the flying foxes of Southeast Asia, which weigh up to 3 ½ pounds (1.6 kilograms) and have wingspans of 79 inches (2 meters).

Mexican free-tailed bat.

"HAND WINGS"

All bats belong to the scientific order Chiroptera, a name coming from two Greek words meaning "hand" and "wing." A bat's hand is similar to a human hand with its four long fingers and a smaller thumb. The difference is that the bat's hand is enormous compared to the size of its body. If you were a bat, your fingers would be nearly as long as your total body height!

The long thin bones of the bat's fingers are like the spokes of an umbrella. They support the thin double layer of skin that forms the bat's wings. In flight the skin is stretched tight between the wing bones, but when the bat is at rest, the skin puckers up and shrinks like a deflated balloon. The bat's short thumb bones extend forward from its wrist and end in a sharp claw.

The size and shape of a bat's wings depend on its species and life-style. Some bats, such as the big brown bats, have short broad wings that are good for quick turns and changes of direction. Other bats, like the Mexican free-tails, have longer, narrower wings better suited for long-distance flying.

Bats use their wings for flight, as nets or baskets to catch and hold prey, and, with some species, to wrap themselves in when resting.

15

Life-sized museum model of a gray-headed flying fox.

The Chiroptera order is divided into two suborders, Megachiroptera, meaning "big hand wing," and Microchiroptera, meaning "small hand wing." The Megachiroptera suborder includes just one scientific family made up of 150 species. All of these are large bats that eat fruit and flower nectar. Members of this suborder are found only in tropical regions of Africa, India, Southeast Asia, the East Indies, and Australia. These are places where fruit is plentiful year-round. The bats often roost in trees, and when they are at rest with their wings folded around themselves, they look something like small dark umbrellas. Some of the large fruit-eating bats are also called flying foxes, because their narrow snouts and pointed ears resemble those of foxes. The Megachiroptera bats are not found in the Americas, and for that reason they are sometimes called Old World bats. Most bats in this group have claws on their second fingers in addition to those on their thumbs.

A western pipistrelle, with its wings folded and tucked next to its furry body.

Forty-three species of bats are found in North America, and all are in the Microchiroptera suborder. Worldwide, this suborder includes about 750 species. Most species in this suborder are small, and most are insect eaters. The largest Microchiroptera bat is the false vampire bat, which has a wingspan of 3 feet (1 meter). It preys on birds, other bats, rodents, lizards, and frogs.

The Microchiroptera suborder is a widely diverse group of bats that is subdivided into seventeen scientific families. Big brown and little brown bats are plain-nosed bats, the largest of all bat families, with approximately 320 different species. Other North American bats in this family include the pipistrelles, evening bats, and red bats.

Mexican free-tailed bats are one of more than eighty species in the free-tailed bat family. Free-tailed bats are so named because their short blunt tails extend beyond the skin between the body and the hind legs. (This thin skin, called the interfemoral membrane, is attached to the tailbones of some bats.)

New World leaf-nosed bats are another large family, with 123 species. All of the bats in this group have fleshy growths on their faces. The New World leaf-nosed bat family includes the famous blood-eating vampire bats. There are three species of vampire bats, and they are all found only in Central and South America.

Hog-nosed, slit-faced, and mouse-tailed bats are the common names of a few of the other families in the Microchiroptera suborder, and they indicate the wide variety in this group.

California leaf-nosed bat.

Vampire bats.

A big brown bat holds on with its thumb claws as it crawls across bark.

WHERE BATS LIVE

Bats live on every continent except Antarctica. Many species are found in warm tropical forests, but bats also live in swamps, deserts, grasslands, and even in cold northern regions. When bats are not flying about, they find secluded resting places called *roosts*. Bats roost in a variety of locations, including caves, mines, tunnels, tall trees, bushes, old buildings, and attics. Because most bats are small, they can slip through cracks and tiny openings to reach these concealed roosts. Some bats are solitary, while others roost together in huge colonies. In such a colony each square foot (.09 square meter) may contain as many as 300 bats!

Bats often live in dark places, and most species have dark skin and fur without distinctive markings. (Bright or patterned markings are not useful because they are hard to see in the dark.) A few bats, however, have spots, stripes, or brightly colored fur. Many of these brightly colored bats roost in trees. Scientists think that their markings may make them blend into the dappled light of their surroundings and help them hide from predators.

Although bats usually get from one place to another by flying, they sometimes move about in their roosts by crawling on all fours. They use the sharp thumb claws on their wings to pull themselves forward. Their thumbs help them grip, so they can move easily across rough surfaces, such as cave walls or tree bark.

Some bats must climb to a branch or other high point and then leap off in order to start flying. Others, including vampires, are able to jump up into the air from the ground and take off from there.

A Mexican free-tailed bat has sharp curved claws on its feet.

AN UPSIDE-DOWN WORLD

When a flying bat comes into its roost, it lands feetfirst. Sometimes it lands head up and then turns over to hang by its feet; in other cases it does a somersault in the air and lands already upside down. Except when it flies, a bat spends most of its life head downward, and nearly every part of its body is adapted for activity in this position.

Most bats have highly flexible necks that allow the head to turn and look straight back with the head right side up. Most mammals, including humans, cannot do this.

A bat's toes are long and strong and equipped with sharp curved claws. They can get a tight hold in even the smallest crack or crevice in a rock wall. When a bat hangs upside

A Mexican free-tailed bat at rest.

down, its weight helps to lock its toes into a firm grip so that even when the bat goes to sleep, it is in no danger of falling.

A bat uses its feet and teeth to clean itself. It can do this while hanging by one foot and using the other foot to groom its fur and delicate wing membranes. Bats spend a large part of their waking hours keeping themselves clean.

One thing that bats do right side up is get rid of body waste. Bats urinate and defecate either while flying or by turning right side up in the roost. When many bats roost together for a long time, their solid body waste, or *guano*, piles up on the ground below. In Carlsbad Caverns, the guano is nearly 50 feet (15.2 meters) thick in some places! Bat guano is valuable as fertilizer, and in some places in the world people collect it and use it to nourish their crops.

Most bats are *nocturnal*, meaning they are active mainly at night. Bats spend the day grooming, resting, and sleeping, and in the nighttime hours they search for food.

One advantage of a nocturnal lifestyle is that most predators sleep at night. So do most birds and other animals that might feed on night-flying insects, which means that insect-eating bats usually have little competition for food. A third benefit of nighttime activity is that the air is cooler and more humid then, so bats do not need to work as hard to move about.

A bat uses a great deal of energy when it flies. However, when it is resting, a bat allows its body to cool down and its heart rate to slow, thereby conserving energy to be used later. The Microchiroptera bats are unusual among mammals in their ability to slow down their body processes. These periods of low-energy resting are called *torpor*. Many of the smaller bats in this suborder go into torpor on a daily basis, resting by day and resuming full activity at night. On the other hand, most of the Megachiroptera bats are able to maintain a constant warm body temperature and do not go into torpor. In cool weather, they wrap themselves with their wings to trap heat in their fur. When the weather is hot, they can fan themselves with their large wings to get cool.

Large eyes help Indian fruit bats see at night (left). Wrapped in dark wings, they rest by day (above).

DO BATS SEE?

The saying "blind as a bat" is another mistaken idea about bats. All bats can see, and many can see particularly well in dim light. Most fruit-eating bats find their way and locate food almost entirely by sight. Their large bulging eyes are a sign of their excellent vision. All of the Megachiroptera bats are able to see colors, an ability that the Microchiroptera bats do not have. They may also use their sense of smell to locate ripe fruit.

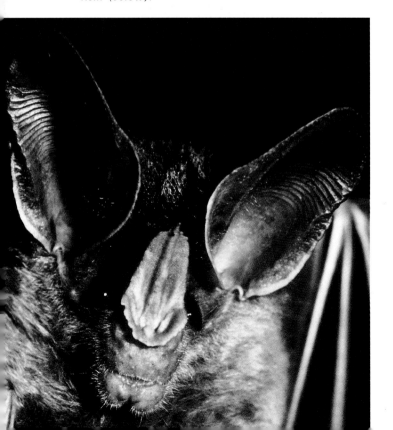

A big brown bat opens its mouth to echolocate (above). The large ears of the woolly false vampire bat help it hear (below).

"SEEING" WITH SOUND

Many bats find their way around and locate prey by using their sense of hearing. They send out streams of high-pitched sounds and listen for echoes bouncing off objects around them. Bats use the echoes to determine the location, distance, and size of these objects. Echoes also give bats information about the texture and shape of things and, in some cases, even about which insects are edible and which are not. This technique of identifying objects in the environment is called *echolocation.*

Echolocation is an ideal way to locate moving prey because it allows a predator to follow an animal as it changes position. All of the Microchiroptera are able to echolocate well. The Megachiroptera, on the other hand, cannot echolocate, or do so in a limited way. Those that are able to echolocate make clicking noises with their tongues rather than vocal sounds.

Bats echolocate both at rest and in flight. Some bats send out sounds

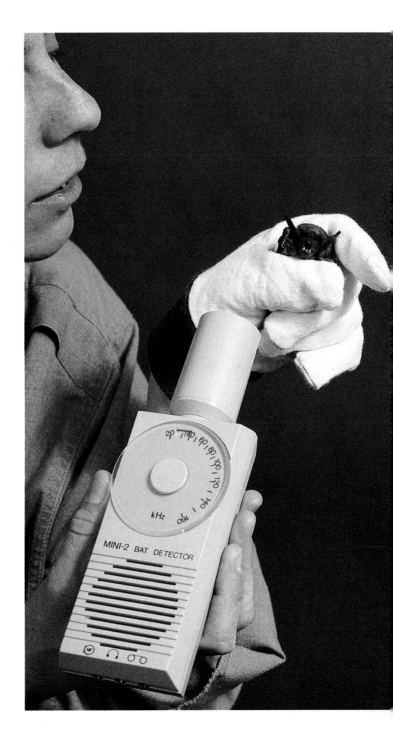

through their mouths, so they fly with their mouths open. Other bats send out sounds through their noses. Bats that echolocate in this way often have special flaps and folds of skin on their faces called *nose leaves.* Scientists think that nose leaves help bats to direct and focus their sound pulses.

Most of the extremely high-pitched noises that bats make are above the range of human hearing. They are called *ultrasounds.* People who study bats often use a device called a bat detector that can hear and measure ultrasounds. The bat detector changes the high-pitched calls to sounds that people can hear. It can help locate the bat and sometimes even help identify the bat's species.

Most bats have large ears compared to the size of their bodies. Big ears help an animal to hear better because they trap more sounds. To see for yourself, put your hand behind your ear to make it bigger and listen to the difference in how much you can hear.

A lesser long-nosed bat spreads pollen as it feeds on the nectar of cactus flowers (museum model).

BAT FOOD

All of the Megachiroptera and some of the Microchiroptera eat fruit, nectar, or pollen. Fruit bats help many plants grow in the world's deserts and rain forests by pollinating them and spreading their seeds.

All flowering plants produce pollen and use it to make seeds. With many plant species, the pollen needs to be spread from one flower to another. Bats that drink nectar often brush against the insides of flowers, and small grains of pollen stick to their fur. The bats then carry the pollen to other flowers as they continue to feed.

More than 500 kinds of plants rely on bats to pollinate them. Some of the fruits that are pollinated by bats include bananas, papayas, mangoes, and avocados. Desert plants such as the saguaro and organ-pipe cactuses of the southwestern United States also rely on bats for pollination.

A short-faced fruit bat eating a slice of banana.

Fruit-eating bats help rain forests in another way. Bats often drop seeds as they carry fruit to their roosts. Seeds also fall to the ground in their droppings. By spreading seeds, bats help plants get started in new locations. Bats are responsible for dispersing up to 95 percent of the seeds needed for the growth of new trees in tropical rain forests.

Evening flight of Mexican free-tailed bats.

Seventy percent of all bats are insect eaters. They eat moths, beetles, flies, mosquitoes, and many other kinds of insects. Bats help farmers by killing millions of harmful insects that would otherwise destroy their crops. Scientists estimate that the 20 million Mexican free-tailed bats that live in Bracken Cave in Texas eat up to 250 tons (227.3 metric tons) of insects each night as they forage over the surrounding countryside. A bat has a huge appetite for its small size and can eat from one-quarter to one-half its body weight in insects in one night. Bats digest their food rapidly and can fill their stomachs several times nightly.

Bats usually begin their search for insects in the early evening. In places where large numbers of bats roost together, the nightly bat flight looks like a large dark cloud. Bats may fly 30 miles (48.4 kilometers) or more each night to find food.

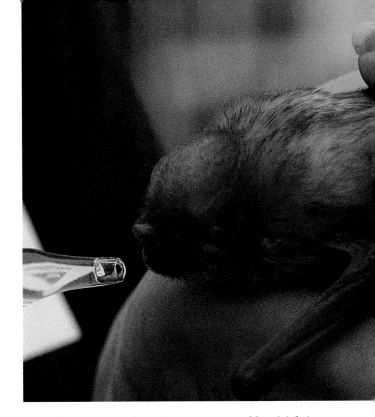

A big brown bat (left) uses sharp teeth to eat a mealworm. An eyedropper is used to give water to a red bat (right).

Many bats catch insects in the air, but they also pluck them off leaves and branches or find them on the ground. Sometimes bats grab the insects with their mouths. In other cases they use their wings or membranes around their tails to scoop up and trap the insects. Captive bats like Tad and Gus are usually fed a diet of mealworms, the larval stage of flour beetles.

A bat's teeth and the shape of its mouth are adapted to the type of food it eats. Fruit bats have large flat teeth that are good for grinding pulpy fruit. Insect-eating bats like Tad and Gus have large jagged teeth in the sides of their mouths that slice against each other like tiny knives. These are ideal for cutting and grinding an insect's hard outer skeleton into small pieces.

Although most bats eat insects, fruit, or plants, a few species are meat eaters and catch small animals such as fish, frogs, mice, or birds. They have developed special techniques for catching their prey. A fish-eating bat, for instance, glides low over the sur-

A pallid bat grabs a scorpion (museum model).

face of a pond and grabs small fish with the sharp talons on its feet. The pallid bat, which lives in the deserts of the southwestern United States, sometimes lands on the ground and stalks scorpions, grasshoppers, and beetles.

Only three bat species drink blood. The common vampire bat feeds mainly on the blood of cattle, horses, mules, and other domestic livestock. The hairy-legged and white-winged vampires feed mainly on the blood of birds. Vampire bats feed by piercing the skin of their sleeping victim and then licking the oozing blood with their tongues. Despite their terrible reputation, created by the fictional Dracula stories, real vampire bats rarely attack people.

Like other animals, bats need water to live. Some bats get enough moisture from their food and do not need to drink. Most bats live close to a source of water such as a stream, marsh, or lake. Bats drink by flying low over the surface of the water and scooping some up into their mouths.

BATS IN WINTER

In North America and other places where the weather turns cold in winter, many bats go into caves, hollow trees, old buildings, and other sheltered places, where they hibernate until spring. Hibernation is a state of inactivity during which the animal's heartbeat, breathing, and other body functions slow down. During hibernation a bat's heart rate slows from its summer rate of 400 beats a minute to below 25 beats per minute. In some cases its body temperature drops below freezing.

A hibernating bat lives on stored fat built up from the food it ate during the previous summer. During periods of warm weather a bat may wake up and eat and drink briefly. Some bats, however, may remain in a state of hibernation for five months or more.

The bats' winter homes are called *hibernacula.* Bats often hibernate in caves, because the air inside is cool and moist and the temperature stays fairly constant. The humidity is important, since the bats do not drink for four or five months, and without moisture in the air they would dry up.

Instead of hibernating in winter, some species of bats migrate, or travel, between their summer and winter homes. As long as they have a good food supply, they can remain active year-round. Many Mexican free-tailed bats use caves in the southwestern United States in summer and spend the winter in central Mexico. These bats migrate as many as 1,500 miles (2,419.4 kilometers) each way. Bats are strong fliers, and if they are flying with the wind, they can attain speeds of 60 miles (96.8 kilometers) per hour. Some tropical fruit bats also migrate as they search for new sources of ripe fruit.

BABY BATS

Mating behavior varies greatly among the many species of bats, but with all bats, a male does not help care for or feed the young and generally leaves the female after mating.

In North America, baby bats are usually born in late spring or early summer. A baby bat is called a *pup,* and although some bats produce twins or occasionally even three or four pups, most raise only one baby a year.

Big brown bats that live in eastern North America often have twins, whereas bats of the same species that live in the West have only one pup each year. Little brown bats and Mexican free-tailed bats usually have just one pup.

A baby bat is normally born bottom first and emerges as its mother hangs upside down. However, in some bat species, such as the little brown bat, the mother bat turns right side up to give birth and catches the baby in her tail membrane. Most baby bats are hairless at birth, but within a few days their hair begins to grow.

Baby bats are enormous compared to newborns of other mammals. A bat pup may be nearly one-third the size of its mother, or the equivalent of a 40-pound (18.2-kilogram) human baby! The newborn bat is helpless in most respects, but it is an expert in hanging on to its roost or its mother and can cling to her even when she flies. The young bat uses its feet to grasp its mother's hair and its mouth to hang on to one of her two teats. A bat is born with tiny milk teeth that help it hold on. These teeth are replaced with adult teeth when the bat is about three weeks old.

A female little brown bat nurses her pup.

Female little brown bats and their babies form nursery colonies in buildings and hollow trees. Although these groups may range in size from a dozen to a thousand bats, they are small compared to some of the nursery colonies of Mexican free-tailed bats, which number in the millions. Mexican free-tailed bats mate in the spring, and in the southern United States the females give birth to their young in late June and early July. Female bats often return to the same nursery site year after year. Scientists who studied droppings and other bat remains in Carlsbad Caverns discovered that bats have been using that site for 17,000 years!

The large fruit bats often carry their pups with them while they forage, but insect-eating bats usually leave their babies behind when they go out hunting for food. A mother Mexican free-tailed bat leaves her pup for the first time when it is a few hours old. She places her baby in a cluster of other young bats, where it stays until she returns several hours later. When the mother comes back to the cave, she calls out to her youngster. Each bat has its own distinctive sound, and a mother bat is able to recognize her baby's cry even when there are hundreds of other bats nearby. When the mother bat gets close to her baby, she smells it carefully to make sure that it is hers. After letting her pup nurse, she cleans and grooms it.

With most bat species, a mother nurses her pup for one to three months. The mother bat's rich milk helps her baby to grow rapidly. Although a baby bat's wings are tiny at first, they grow fast. By the time a Mexican free-tailed bat is about three weeks old, it can fly. At first the young bat is clumsy and cannot echolocate, maneuver, or land with the skill of an adult. Learning to fly is especially difficult because the young bat must do it in the dark!

The first few weeks are the most dangerous time in a young bat's life, and it is at this age that many bats perish. Young bats that survive the hazards of growing up may live for many years. Bats are long-lived animals for their size, and some species live to be more than thirty years old.

PREDATORS OF BATS

The ability to fly safeguards bats from most land-dwelling predators. Animals such as snakes, however, can climb to the places where bats roost, and other animals, such as opossums, raccoons, and skunks, prey on bats that fall to the ground. The main hunters of bats, though, are hawks and owls, because they can catch bats in the air.

These birds of prey often wait outside the places where bats roost and catch them as they emerge at dusk. Owls, which have excellent sight and hearing, also hunt bats at night. Swooping on silent wings, they surprise their prey. Small bats may be preyed upon by larger, meat-eating bats as well.

A single bat is so small that it does not make a full meal for a large animal. Most predators do not hunt bats unless it is possible to catch many of them in a short period of time. Bats are most active on moonless nights or when the moon is covered by clouds. When the night is dark, it is more difficult for predators to see them.

Great horned owls (left), snakes (above), and opossums (below) are some of the animals that prey on bats.

Mexican free-tailed bat.

ENDANGERED BATS

Nearly 40 percent of the bat species that live in North America are threatened or endangered. These include the gray bat, the big-eared bat, the Indiana bat, and others. Some people kill bats because they believe that they are pests. Bats also suffer when they are disturbed in their roosts, when their food is contaminated by pesticides, and when they cannot find places to roost or enough to eat because the wildlands where they live have been developed for human use.

One way that people are trying to help bats is by protecting them in the places where they roost. Signs and gates at the entrances to caves that bats use for either rearing young or hibernating help prevent people from exploring when bats are around. Mother bats that are disturbed may abandon their babies. And if a hibernating bat wakes up during the winter and does not eat, it uses valuable energy just moving around and staying warm. Every time a hibernating bat is awakened, it loses between ten and thirty days' worth of stored fat. If bats are disturbed even two or three times during their hibernation period, they may not have enough energy to last until spring, and they will die.

The species most commonly found living in bat houses (right) is the big brown bat (below).

Another favorite place for bats to roost is in the attics and rafters of buildings, but tightly insulated houses with modern weatherproofing make this hard to do. A relatively new idea for helping bats is the use of bat houses. Like birdhouses, bat houses provide places for bats to live when natural roosting sites may not be available. They can be mounted on poles or on the sides of buildings and provide an opportunity for people to observe bats in their own neighborhoods. The bats, in turn, help keep bothersome insects under control. At least 200 bats can easily fit in a bat house just 2 feet (.62 meter) high.

Bats in many other parts of the world are also at risk. The destruction of rain forests, a habitat for fruit bats, is the main cause for the decline of these bats. In some countries, fruit bats are also hunted for food, and at least one species has become extinct for this reason.

RULING THE NIGHT SKY

Without help from people, the number of bats in the world will continue to decline. Many organizations involved with protecting wildlife are working to help bats. The largest of these is Bat Conservation International, directed by bat scientist Merlin Tuttle. Through public education, the promotion of laws that help protect bats and the places where they live, and the sponsorship of research about bats, such groups are trying to make the world a better place for bats.

People have been curious about bats for thousands of years. Pictures of bats are found in ancient Egyptian tombs, on medieval coats of arms, and on old pottery from China. People around the world have many different views of bats, ranging from fear and superstition to worship and admiration.

Bats like Gus and Tad are helping us understand more about these animals and their role in the balance of nature. Bats are mysterious and fascinating, and as long as they can find food and places to live, they will continue to be rulers of the night sky.

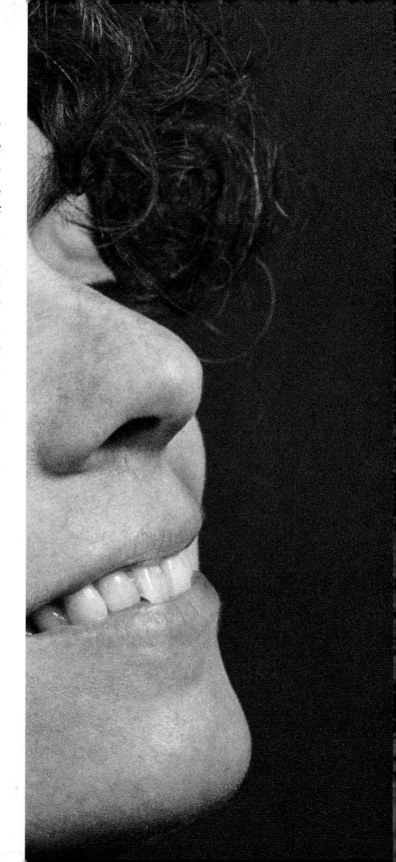

INDEX

Photographs are in **boldface.**